PROVOCATION, PRAYER & PRAISE.

by
Oluwakemi O. Ola-Ojo.

Unless otherwise indicated, all Old Testament Scripture quotations are taken from the King James Version [KJV] of the Holy Bible and the Living Bible [LB], Copyright © 1971 by Tyndale House Publishers, Wheaton, Illinois.

1st Printing 2004 ISBN 1-4120-2690-3
2nd Edition 2009

Provocation, Prayer and Praise
ISBN 978-0-9557898-3-0

Copyright © 2009 by Oluwakemi O. Ola-Ojo
PO Box 48424
London
SE15 2YL
United Kingdom

Published by Protokos Publishers
Cover design by Prexng@yahoo.com
Author's Picture by Hill Stanton

Printed by
Lightning Source.
Milton Keynes, UK

ALL RIGHTS RESERVED
No part of this publication may be reproduced, stored in a retrieval system, or transmitted in any form or by any means without prior permission of the Publisher.

For couples who are trusting God for the

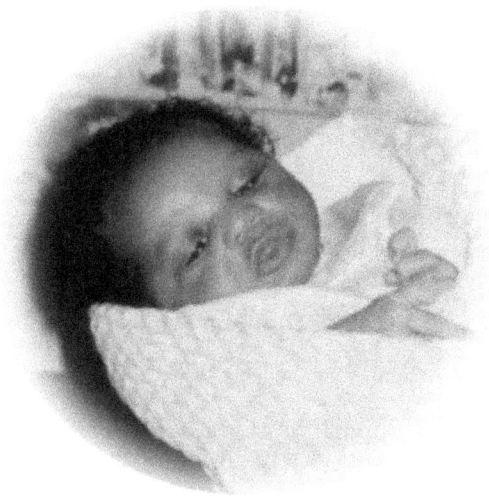

fruit of the womb.

ACKNOWLEDGEMENT

God is to be praised for the insight He gave me into the story shared in this book.

Thanks to Baby Joshua and his parents for the use of his picture in this book.

The thoughtfulness and kindness of my family and friends has been thankfully received.

Thanks to Mrs Olabisi Omilabu for editing this second edition.

I thank Gospel Publishing House, USA for the use of the song, What a Friend We Have in Jesus. This book, like the previous ones, has enjoyed the unique cover design by Prex Nigeria Limited to whose management and staff I am most grateful.

I also appreciate the staff of Protokos Publishers for helping to make my dreams come through in publishing and marketing this book.

ABOUT THE BOOK

Provocation, Prayer & Praise is an insightful and wellpresented handbook that looks at infertility from a woman's perspective. A good read and a must read for every man!"
Rev Chuks Anierobi, CEO,
The Shepherd's Ministries

"This book roots lasting principles within the context of one woman's story". A story which at every point becomes every woman's story or maybe even every person's story. The story of what to do, how to be and what to say in the face of trouble, testing, trial and trauma. A story that examines provocations that are commonplace and prayers and praises which though uncommon in the life experience of many ought to become the record of our response to the trouble that
life represents.

A reading of this book will help every one of us formulate an adequate and appropriate response. It reminds us that we are required to pray about everything and give thanks in all situations."

Pastor Ode Andrew Eyeoyibo, DIRECTOR,
Epignosia Ministries

CONTENTS

Acknowledgement — IV
About the Book — V
Foreword — 7
Introductions to 1st & 2nd Editions. — 10

Chapter 1
Give God Your All — 19

Chapter 2
Rescued at 'Quarter to Shame' — 43

Chapter 3
The Power of Prayer — 52

Chapter 4
The Sovereignty of God — 61
Poems – *"My Unlimited God"*
"God's Gift You can never Buy"
"The Lord is Working"
"Who Are You listening to in that Situation?"
"My faith is being put to test".

Song – *"What a Friend we have in Jesus"* — 85

Opportunity to Become a Christian — 87
Support Group — 89
Useful Addresses /Web Sites — 98

FOREWORD

We live in the twenty-first century, the information technology age where man is exploring more than ever before new frontiers in science. Mankind now lives in a global village made possible by cyberspace communication and undertakes daring adventures within and beyond our solar system. It's a time when medical science has made tremendous advancement in many areas including the treatment of infertility. Science has successfully diagnosed many of the causes of infertility and many people have benefited from sophisticated procedures.

However, even as mankind crosses the threshold of genetic manipulation, we cannot but acknowledge the supernatural intervention of God in breaking the bondage of barrenness and infertility.

It is not a contest between faith and medicine. It is a cooperation. Sometimes faith enhances the success of scientific procedures and most times where science ends, faith begins.

FOREWORD

In Ruth 4:13, it is written, *"...the Lord gave her conception..."* God gives conception despite medical reports and other circumstances because He is God and He is supernatural.

He made Sarah to conceive at ninety years old, Elizabeth and the wife of Manoah conceived long after menopause. The Lord Jesus Christ was born by a virgin who found favour with God. God is the same yesterday, today and forever. He said, *"Let there be light"* also said, *"Be fruitful and multiply."*

As long as nothing can break the covenant of day and night then nothing can stop God from giving conception to the barren and making them joyful parents.

In Exodus 23:25-26 and Deuteronomy 7:12-15 God explicitly reminds us of His desire that we be fruitful; He even promised that our animals will not be barren. How much more precious is a child of God made in His own image than livestock?

The key therefore is being rightly positioned to receive from God and that is what this book is all about. Sister Kemi Ojo, a medical professional with many years of experience writes with deep insight and compassion this anointed book to help position us for God's miracle touch. In this exposition of Hannah's encounter with the God with whom all things are possible, she clearly

shows how to obtain God's favour. Hannah did not just pray and believe God; her motive was right and godly. She exercised her faith, her countenance changed, her attitude changed, and then the Lord remembered her.
As you read this book, God will remember you in Jesus' precious name.

He who *"...raises the poor out of the dunghill and make them sit among the princes of the people..."* will raise you up from shame and affliction. He will fulfill your hearts desire and crown you with glory.

Rev. Peter Kayode Adegbie.
(CEO, Golden Pot Media)

Introduction to the 1st Edition

This book is based on 1 Samuel chapters 1 – 2:10. verse 1-28 and chapter 2, verse 1-10. It is worthwhile to read verses in a translation that is easy for you to understand so you can better comprehend and have more insight once you begin reading the book.

It is complimentary to my other book, 'The Christian and Infertility'. The above portion of scripture clearly shows that our problems are not new and someone else has been through it before in another age, at another time and another generation. Here, out of many others that can be found in the Bible, we have one example of how to overcome the pain and distress of childlessness.

This is a story of a man and his two wives, one able to conceive and the other barren. The lessons however can be applied to any situation that makes anyone incomplete, unfulfilled or less than others. The God who gives children is able to meet that need, and solve that issue in your life where you are constantly being challenged, harassed and provoked.

My desire is that the words of this book will TAKE you from a place of hopelessness and helplessness to faith in a God who sees and knows.

Introduction to the 2nd Edition

God is to be praised for the many testimonies that have been received since the first publication of this book. In this second edition, I have added at the end of each chapter some spaces for writing your personal thoughts.

For those who do not have a Bible within reach and to make reading easy and focussed, I have included the New King James Version of the story just before the first chapter of this book. Also, more encouraging poems and useful addresses/ website addresses have been added.

Friend, God is waiting to hear from you with regards to whatever is provoking you, in Him and through Him, you will laugh last and laugh best

PROVOCATION, PRAYER & PRAISE.

1 Samuel 1 – 2:11

*from New King James Version
(NKJV) Copyright © 1982
by Thomas Nelson, Inc.*

1 Now there was a certain man of Ramathaim Zophim, of the mountains of Ephraim, and his name was Elkanah the son of Jeroham, the son of Elihu,[a] the son of Tohu,[b] the son of Zuph, an raimite.
2 And he had two wives: the name of one was Hannah, and the name of the other Peninnah. Peninnah had children, but Hannah had no children.
3 This man went up from his city yearly to worship and sacrifice to the Lord of hosts in Shiloh. Also the two sons of Eli, Hophni and Phinehas, the priests of the Lord, were there.
4 And whenever the time came for Elkanah to make an offering, he would give portions to Peninnah his wife and to all her sons and daughters.
5 But to Hannah he would give a double portion, for he loved Hannah, although the Lord had closed her womb.

***6** And her rival also provoked her severely, to make her miserable, because the Lord had closed her womb.*

***7** So it was, year by year, when she went up to the house of the Lord, that she provoked her; therefore she wept and did not eat.*

***8** Then Elkanah her husband said to her, "Hannah, why do you weep? Why do you not eat? And why is your heart grieved? Am I not better to you than ten sons?"*

***9** So Hannah arose after they had finished eating and drinking in Shiloh. Now Eli the priest was sitting on the seat by the doorpost of the tabernacle[c] of the Lord.*

***10** And she was in bitterness of soul, and prayed to the Lord and wept in anguish.*

***11** Then she made a vow and said, "O LORD of hosts, if You will indeed look on the affliction of Your maidservant and remember me, and not forget Your maidservant, but will give Your maidservant a male child, then I will give him to the LORD all the days of his life, and no razor shall come upon his head."*

***12** And it happened, as she continued praying before the LORD, that Eli watched her mouth. 13 Now Hannah spoke in her heart; only her lips moved, but her voice was not heard. Therefore Eli thought she was drunk.*

***14** So Eli said to her, "How long will you be drunk? Put your wine away from you!"*
***15** But Hannah answered and said, "No, my lord, I am a woman of sorrowful spirit. I have drunk neither wine nor intoxicating drink, but have poured out my soul before the LORD. **16** Do not consider your maidservant a wicked woman,[d] for out of the abundance of my complaint and grief I have spoken until now."*
***17** Then Eli answered and said, "Go in peace, and the God of Israel grant your petition which you have asked of Him."*
***18** And she said, "Let your maidservant find favor in your sight." So the woman went her way and ate, and her face was no longer sad.*
***19** Then they rose early in the morning and worshiped before the LORD, and returned and came to their house at Ramah. And Elkanah knew Hannah his wife, and the LORD remembered her. **20** So it came to pass in the process of time that Hannah conceived and bore a son, and called his name Samuel,[e]saying, "Because I have asked for him from the LORD."*
***21** Now the man Elkanah and all his house went up to offer to the LORD the yearly sacrifice and his vow.*
***22** But Hannah did not go up, for she said to her husband, "Not until the child is weaned; then*

I will take him, that he may appear before the LORD and remain there forever."

23 *So Elkanah her husband said to her, "Do what seems best to you; wait until you have weaned him. Only let the LORD establish His[f] word." Then the woman stayed and nursed her son until she had weaned him.*

24 *Now when she had weaned him, she took him up with her, with three bulls,[g] one ephah of flour, and a skin of wine, and brought him to the house of the LORD in Shiloh. And the child was young.*

25 *Then they slaughtered a bull, and brought the child to Eli. 26 And she said, "O my lord! As your soul lives, my lord, I am the woman who stood by you here, praying to the LORD. 27 For this child I prayed, and the LORD has granted me my petition which I asked of Him.*

28 *Therefore I also have lent him to the LORD; as long as*

he lives he shall be lent to the LORD." So they worshiped the LORD there.

1 Samuel 2: 1-11:

***1** And Hannah prayed and said: "My heart rejoices in the LORD; My horn[a] is exalted in the LORD. I smile at my enemies, Because I rejoice in Your salvation.*
***2** "No one is holy like the LORD, For there is none besides You, Nor is there any rock like our God.*
***3** "Talk no more so very proudly; Let no arrogance come from your mouth, For the LORD is the God of knowledge; And by Him actions are weighed.*
***4** "The bows of the mighty men are broken, And those who stumbled are girded with strength.*
***5** Those who were full have hired themselves out for bread, And the hungry have ceased to hunger. Even the barren has borne seven, And she who has many children has become feeble.*
***6** "The LORD kills and makes alive; He brings down to the grave and brings up.*
***7** The LORD makes poor and makes rich; He brings low and lifts up.*
***8** He raises the poor from the dust And lifts the beggar from the ash heap, To set them among princes And make them inherit the throne of*

glory. "For the pillars of the earth are the LORD's, And He has set the world upon them.

__9__ He will guard the feet of His saints, But the wicked shall be silent in darkness. "For by strength no man shall prevail.

__10__ The adversaries of the LORD shall be broken in pieces; From heaven He will thunder against them. The LORD will judge the ends of the earth. "He will give strength to His king, And exalt the horn of His anointed."

__11__ Then Elkanah went to his house at Ramah. But the child ministered to the LORD before Eli the priest.

1

GIVE GOD YOUR ALL

This is the story of a man from Ramathaimzophim, a Zuphite from the hill country of Ephraim, whose name was Elkanah.

Elkanah had two wives - Peninnah and Hannah. Peninnah had children but Hannah had none. From this man seeds from his loins gave children to one woman but not to the other.

From Psalms 127:3-5, we know that children are a gift from God and that it is good to have many. Thus, as to the reason why Hannah did not have children, we do not know, but we do know that only God gives children.

CAUSES OF INFERTILITY

From the medical perspective, these are the broad classifications or causes of infertility:

I) **Male factors**

There are three main reasons for infertility in men. These could be pathological, medical or immunological.

Pathological reasons means there is an underlying cause

a. Befective sperm production (hypospermia and azospermia
b. Congenital undescended testis
c. Medical conditions – big hydrocele, varicocele
d. Infections like mumps (viral) and bacterial infections after puberty
e. Chronic debilitating disease, malnutrition, heavy smoking and alcoholism
f. Diabetes and thyroid problems
g. Genetic problems like Klinrfelter's syndrome (XXY)

Medical reasons are:

a. Frequent x-ray exposures and radiotherapy
b. Anti-cancer drugs
c. Certain drugs including some anti convulsion drugs

Immunological reasons

a. *Auto-antibodies* - this is caused by some disorders in the man's immune system. For some reason the body develops antibodies against its own cells. In this case, the man's antibodies destroy his own sperms and the wife may also develop antibodies against the husband's sperms.

b. *Obstruction to the tube travelled by sperms*: secondary to infections such as gonorrhoea or following surgical hernia operations.

II) Female factors - these include the following:
a. Congenital abnormalities which may affect the uterus or and ovary.
b. A woman who has never menstruated in her life due to a genetic defect such as Turners syndrome.
c. Early cessation of menstruation otherwise dermoid, ovarian teratoma which could be the cystic or solid type.
d. Ovulation defects e.g. hyperprolactinaemia.
e. Tubal problems such as blocked tubes, fluid or pus filled tubes otherwise referred to as hydrosalpinx, pyosalpinx.
f. Pelvic inflammatory disease (PID).
g. Space occupied lesions in the endometrial cavity such as fibroids or polyps.
h. A very rare situation in which there is incompatibility between the sperm and the woman's egg.

III) Combined factors – that is, sub-fertility may be due to some factors in both the man and woman, e.g.

low sperm count in the man and polycystic ovary in the woman.

IV) Unexplained factors - this is when after a battery of tests no medical cause could be found in the couple for sub-fertility yet the woman is unable to conceive.

Since Peninnah had children, the infertility of Elkanah and Hannah as a couple would be classified medically today as due to a female factor.

THE PLACE OF WORSHIP

Year after year Elkanah went up from his town to worship and sacrifice to the LORD at Shiloh. Eli was the high priest at that time and his two sons were the ministering priests.

This visit was in obedience to God's instruction as seen in Deuteronomy 16:16-17 where God commands that three times a year all males shall appear before Him in the place which He chooses. This was supposed to be a time of joy and celebration, no wonder the Psalmist said, *"I was glad when they said to me let us go into the house of the LORD"* Psalms 122:1.

Mankind was made to worship God and fellowship with Him. Thank God you and I need not make a yearly trip to some place to worship God again. Jesus paid the ultimate sacrifice on the cross of Calvary for all of Mankind's sins once and for all. For those who have accepted Him as their LORD and SAVIOUR, we can rejoice in this ultimate sacrifice. We are now able to approach God in worship anywhere and anytime in Spirit and in truth [John 4:23 – 24].

According to the custom in the days of Elkanah, every member of the family was meant to appear before the LORD. Hannah could have stopped going to Shiloh year after year after all she had no issue; God had not blessed her with the fruit of the womb. But like Job, she probably said in her heart among other things, *'Even though HE slay me yet I will trust Him'* [Job 13:15]. Are there not people today who will stop praying, singing, sharing with others and stop going to church because of their problems? This sometimes may be due to frustration, bitterness of spirit, and un-forgiveness of other's insensitivity towards them or simply a total lack of faith in God. Our faith, loyalty and obedience to God will sustain us in times like this.

There are often times of celebration in the year that can prove to be very difficult for some. For example, Mother's day or Father's day - for the orphan, children in care, children and adult in broken marriages, childless couples, mothers or fathers whose child or children are no more or are in one form of trouble or the other (prison), abused or neglected children, unwanted children who have now been adopted. Even Christmas day and the days leading to a New Year - for the lonely, poor, sick, elderly, foreigners too far away from their families, singles, those who are shut in, etc. During such seasons and for such people, we must be very sensitive to help them in any way that we can. While this will not change their situation, we can at least help them to focus on something a bit more exciting than their present condition.

When they got to Shiloh, Elkanah would give portions of meat to Peninnah and her children and to Hannah he would give a double portion because he loved her. It must have been a difficult time for Elkanah as the wife he loved was childless. Jacob had the same problem with Rachel [Genesis 29:30-31; 30:1-2]. It was a situation in which Elkanah was helpless and unable to help his much loved wife Hannah. Nothing can satisfy a barren womb, not even a double portion of meat for sacrifice, nor more love from Elkanah [Proverbs 30:15–16].

High levels of anxiety and emotional distress often accompany infertility in a couple. For Hannah it was a time of shame, reproach, crying and wailing and who knows what else.

The society in which we live today is woven around the family and often it may be difficult for a childless couple to attend family celebrations as they are often reminded of their infertility, consciously by insensitive comments or acts and unconsciously through ignorance or careless comments.

GOD HAS THE FINAL SAY

Hannah's barrenness was from the LORD! The Bible says, *"...but the Lord had shut up her womb."* How could this be when God said as He created the world, *"Be fruitful and multiply, fill the earth and subdue it"* [Genesis 1:27-28]?

God does not contradict Himself. See Jeremiah 29:11 as proof of this.

Personally, I think Hannah's inability to conceive was for a purpose, a time and about a season according to the time of life which only God knew. Each person needs to find the source of his or her problems. Not every problem stems from personal sin, an ancestral yoke, Satan's oppression or as in Hannah's case her barrenness was from God.

Another example of this is that of the boy born blind whom Jesus healed [John 9:1-3]. Only God can open a womb He has sealed, no doctor or infertility treatment can. Whatever the source of barrenness and whatever the problem, God is able to deal with it. Jesus has been given a name above all names and at the mention of that name every knee must bow. [Philippians 2:9-11]. Remember, too, that the scripture says *'I am the LORD thy Healer.'*

THE ENEMY'S STRATEGY TO WEAKEN MAN

Hannah's rival, Peninnah kept provoking her in order to irritate her. This went on year after year. Whenever Hannah went up to the house of the LORD, her rival taunted and provoked her so much that she wept bitterly and would not eat. Intense emotional pain and distress can lead to a loss of appetite. The fact that Hannah's cowife Peninnah had children certainly put an enormous amount of pressure on her in the home. I believe multiple wives are not God's ideal for man plus the fact that God took from Adam one rib and made out of that rib one woman not women. One man, one wife is certainly best. [Genesis 2:21-23]

It is not uncommon to have strife in a family of multiple wives. The world is very competitive, even in families like that of Elkanah's. It would appear that Peninnah was a competitive, insensitive, taunting mate and for whatever reasons derived malicious fun by causing Hannah a lot of misery particularly during times of celebration when Hannah's childlessness was most apparent. How Peninnah could go to such spiteful and vindictive extents indeed makes me wonder. It is not clear what steps Elkanah took to put an end to these torments although we can gather from his statement, *"Hannah, why do you weep? Why do you not eat? And why is your heart grieved? Am I not better to you than ten sons?"* that he loved her dearly, if not deeply. Obviously, this was not much comfort for Hannah neither did it solve the problem.

Peninnah's strategy was to attack Hannah at her weakest and most vulnerable position. Elkanah would give portions to Peninnah and to her sons and daughters and gave only two portions to Hannah. This always brought it home to Hannah, *"I have no children and my husband is trying to make up for it by giving me not one portion but two to worship and sacrifice to the Lord when we get to the temple, where petitions could be made and the priests could intercede for me."* Each year would have renewed the pain somewhat.

It must have been many, many years that Hannah was barren, knowing as we do that it takes nine months before a child can be born and Peninnah had 'sons and daughters', even if she had only two of each, that would have been about four years of barrenness for Hannah and maybe more. She would have watched Peninnah as each pregnancy grew, probably helped her during the birth of each child and then watched the child grow. Where could she hide? What could she do? How much harder could she cry that would change her circumstance? But it is a strategy, which till today is being used by the enemy. Personally I have noticed that when it is about time for my miracle, for things to change for the better for me, the devil will try to disorganise me physically, emotionally and spiritually so that I might miss the blessing from God. Once I realised this wicked strategy, with the help of the HOLY SPIRIT, such a time now is turned to a time of prayer and praise.

It is bad enough to have a problem, which is known to others, worse still it is most painful to be tormented by those who should know better. It is not uncommon for insensitive family members, unfortunately some Christians inclusive, friends or colleagues who should know better to rub salt into one's wounds.

Joy Comes In The Morning

Those who have no problems conceiving and having children should be sensitive and sensible enough not to torment the less fortunate, neither with words or acts. Sometimes the culture or society is unfavourable to the barren, the weak, the disabled etc. For example, there are numerous advertisements here and there about babies and children, which may remind couples with infertility problems of their failure to have children and as such may increase their stress. 'Weeping may endure for the night but joy comes in the morning [Psalms 30:5].' *'One evening after supper, when they were at Shiloh, Hannah went over to the Tabernacle. Eli the priest was sitting at his customary place beside the entrance. She was in deep anguish and was crying bitterly as she prayed to the Lord'* [v.9-10, LB]. There was food and there was drink, everyone including Penninah's children ate and drank but not Hannah and as soon as they had finished eating, she stood up and faced the challenge. In bitterness of soul Hannah wept much and prayed. Well, if the Lord had shut up her womb, the Lord can open it; so asking Him to do so would be the best course of action at this point – that is what Hannah did.

Where and to whom you go seeking for help is vital. The palmist or sorcerer may help but it will come at a great price to you. Besides, it is a sin against God to consult any form of medium [Deuteronomy 18:9-13]. The price has already been paid, Jesus Christ paid it at His death and resurrection, pray to the God who recognises and accepts the price already paid on your behalf, seek help from Him who alone is able to do the impossible.

Fertility treatment cannot open a womb sealed by God; only God can do that. A personal revelation of God is very rewarding at a time like this. Your problem should send you to your knees to pray, not to complain nor murmur against God; not to malign others but to ask God for mercy and removal of the shame and reproach that you feel.

Hannah could have approached Eli the priest but she knew her salvation and help would come from God and not man. I will lift up my eyes to the mountains; from whence shall my help come [Psalms 121:1]? God may use a friend, brother; sister or pastor to speak a word to change the situation but your cry must be to Jehovah God, your Maker and Creator Himself.

Hannah went to the temple with just one prayer request, that which was paramount in her life at the time. She believed that God could answer her if she could just but call to Him. Do you go to Church with your prayer request and the same attitude or do you go just as a routine? Do you believe that God is able to do all things including that which is humanly impossible?

What is faith? It is the confident assurance that something we want is going to happen. It is the certainty that what we hope for is waiting for us, even though we cannot see it up ahead. You can never please God without faith, without depending on him. Anyone who wants to come to God must believe that there is a God and that he rewards those who sincerely look for him [Hebrews 11:1 & 6 LB]. *"For with God nothing will be impossible."* [Luke 1:37 KJV]. For by Him all things were created that are in heaven and that are on earth, visible and invisible, whether thrones or dominions or principalities or powers. All things were created through Him and for Him. [Colossians 1:16 KJV].

God Looks Down From Heaven

Hannah wept and prayed and made a vow: *"O Lord of heaven, if you will look down upon my sorrow and answer my prayer and give me a son, then I will give him back to you, and he'll be yours for his entire lifetime, and his hair shall never be cut."* [v. 11, LB]

Hannah here acknowledges God for whom He is, pleads for God's mercy, asks Him to consider her misery and grant her desire for a son, and then vows to consecrate the son to the Lord. You must acknowledge God for who He is, plead for His mercy and ask. Our merits are insufficient to receive the smallest of God's blessings; only in His mercy can we be recipients of His blessings.

Hannah kept praying to the Lord from her heart not minding Eli's presence. Staying focused during prayer to God is essential. Focus usually tells whether the heart is sincere or not and how important your request is. God will usually acknowledge and grant prayers from a sincere heart.

Eli misunderstood Hannah and rebuked her. Though Eli was the priest then it would seem to me that he lacked the spirit of discernment required to understand what Hannah's mouth movements were without any audible sound. This made Eli the priest insensitive to Hannah's plight. He didn't ask her what the matter was but simply assumed she was drunk. If Hannah was acting like a drunken person would, then Eli would have been right in his assumption but he was wrong because he had become dull of spirit.

Many who may not understand your situation, your grief and your many prayers may make critical judgements about you but like Hannah, you must refuse to take any offence at such. It doesn't just take a friend to be empathetic with your dilemma; it takes one with a discerning heart of compassion, willing to feel your pain with you as God does.

Hannah's answer to Eli's accusation: "Oh, no, sir!" she replied, "I'm not drunk! But I am very sad and I was pouring out my heart to the Lord. Please don't think that I am just some drunken bum!" [v.15-16 LB] – Learn to pour out your soul to God, only He can handle it.

Consulting a man or woman of God may be good but I find that it is best to pour out my heart to God who has the answer to all of my petitions. Elkanah was clearly not sufficiently understanding of Hannah's grief as a result of her barrenness for he asked her among other questions in verse 8 if he was not more to her than ten sons. Elkanah was really asking *"Isn't having me better than having ten sons?"* [LB] The answer in Hannah's heart would have been a loud and resounding NO! Elkanah, Hannah's husband could not give her a child, thus he could not solve the problem. He was only a man. He probably didn't know that truly, nothing could satisfy a barren womb [Proverbs 30:15-16].

Every person around you has a place that they occupy in your life. For example the place and the role of a husband is certainly different from that of a father's and different to that of a brother or uncle and so different from that of a son in a woman's life. Elkanah's assumption that he could be both husband and son to Hannah was grossly inappropriate. To Hannah, Elkanah will always be her husband, not her son.

Perhaps Elkanah probably thought Hannah could appropriate Penninah's children as hers. Unfortunately, that idea does not often work with women particularly where it is the fertility of the woman in question. Even now, in this twenty-first century, depending on whose fertility is in question, the man or the woman, the person tends to feel a lot more vulnerable. Characteristically, men may not understand nor fully appreciate the stress and strain of infertility on their wives. Elkanah continued to have children through Peninnah, he loved Hannah and expressed it, as far as he was concerned, that should have been sufficient enough to make Hannah happy. Barren Israel and Rachel had a similar problem. Read Genesis 29:30-31, 30:1-2.

FINDING FAVOUR WITH GOD

Only God could give Hannah her desire and she was wise in pouring her soul to God. No man can give another person health, joy, abundance of life or peace but God. Make it a habit to turn to God who will in turn send people to bless you. Nothing should be too little to discuss with God. HE is interested and able to help.

Once Hannah had explained her situation to Eli, God used him to pronounce a blessing on Hannah. 'Go in peace [v. 17]. It is in God's peace that you will receive your miracle not in anger, bitterness, jealousy, strife, or unforgiveness, etc. See Psalms 46:10-11.

Hannah's reply was, *"Let your maidservant find favour in your sight..."* [v. 18 this was a proper response to a blessing, one that should be emulated. Saying things like, 'I hope so', 'I will believe when I see', etc. are not words of faith and should not be spoken, not in the heart and neither out of the mouth. 'I believe and I will see' would be a proper response. Negative words and unbelief will stop the flow of God's blessings or even delay its fulfilment. Hannah's countenance changed from this time and she was able to eat again. She started living in the light of God's divine blessing as spoken to Eli the priest.

Knowing that God's revelation needs no second opinion, the only suitable response from her heart was faith in action. No more crying and wailing, no more loss of appetite, no more grief, God had spoken and that was enough. It was enough for Hannah.

The reason for their visit to the temple in Shiloh was over, Elkanah and his family returned home. Hannah put her faith into action, just as there are two sides to any coin, for many of God's promises in His Word, HE has a part to play and the recipient has a part to play too. It was not wise for Hannah to keep herself away from her husband while trusting God for a child. Don't just claim that promise if you are not going to play your required part in it. During Hannah's normal sexual relationship with her husband, God remembered her [v 19-20]. When the root cause of the problem has been identified and dealt with, God will honour His word and remember you in His time.

SHUT THE DOOR AGAINST SIN

Recently a Pastor told a true story of a woman who had fertility problems and none of those she had consulted were able to help her. She was no doubt a Christian from her conversation, yet she was childless. As this Pastor prayed with her, the Lord revealed to him that the cause of her fertility problem was the woman herself. She had always disrespected her husband and not given him the rightful place of honour in the home. The Pastor shared this revelation with her and after repenting of it and correcting the situation by giving her husband due regard and respect, God blessed her with a pregnancy some months later that led to the birth of their son.

Not so long ago, a Christian lady shared this testimony. She had been barren for many years and had consulted many doctors. None could help. Finally she was told she had to go for IVF. (In-Vitro Fertilisation – a method where the woman's egg will be mixed with her husband's sperm in a test tube and the fertilized egg implanted in the woman). This woman wanted a natural conception and as she sought the LORD, she was asked to forgive someone who had offended her in the past. In her state of unforgiveness, she had also kept some documents that were detrimental to this person and was told to destroy them. After much struggling within, she obeyed God.

Within weeks of doing so she conceived and now has a baby boy. Her un-forgiveness kept her from conceiving for many years! Think about this.

The root cause of your problem could be jealousy, anger, unbelief, unforgiveness, impatience, etc. It might also be no fault of yours. Listen, 'God is not a man that He should lie, nor a son of man that He should repent: Has He said, and will He not do it? Or has He spoken, and will He not make it good? Behold God has released a commandment to bless us: Since He has blessed us not even the devil can revoke it.' [Numbers 23:19–23].

What's In A Name?

Hannah conceived, had a son and named him Samuel saying, [meaning] 'Because I asked the LORD for him' [v 20]. As God grants you your desire, you must give Him the glory, the honour, and the praise and reflect this in your rejoicing. Here, this was reflected in the name the child was given and its meaning. There are names you can give to your child that could mean anything but give glory to God. No matter what language you use in naming your children, it is important that you know the meaning of a name before deciding to call your child by that name.

There are numerous books in libraries and using the Internet that can help you in finding the meaning of a name. Don't just call your child a name because you like it. A name is a destiny-defining matter. One other thing that many do not consider is this, each time you call your child by whatever name you give him or her, you are making a confession. For example, if your child is called Belinda (usually a name given to a female child), which means 'snake', you are pronouncing her a snake with all the characteristics of a snake. Think about that. On the other hand, if you name your child Joel which means 'Yahweh is God', you are proclaiming that Yahweh or Jehovah is God and your son answers when you call, saying "Yes", in full agreement to the confession just as Belinda will answer, "Yes", I am a snake with all its characteristics." If you have to change your child's name after reading this book, please do. It will be well worth the effort. God changed Jacob's name to Israel. Jacob [supplanter] to Israel [one who prevails with God], which determined his character to a large extent.

Hannah spent the first few years with her son at home [v.22]. She was a loving, caring and committed mother and was also willing to give him up to the LORD and His service forever. She certainly got her priorities right.

SHOWER YOUR CHILD WITH LOVE

The best things a parent can give to a child are love and time especially in their early and formative years; usually this is up to age five. It has been scientifically proven that a child's character is fully formed by that age and all that is left is a sharpening and smoothening of the developing character traits. Train up the child in the way he should go and when he is old he will not depart from it [Proverbs 22:6].

Elkanah said to Hannah "Do what seems best to you; wait until you have weaned him. Only let the Lord establish His Word [v. 23]. There was agreement between Elkanah and Hannah in the upbringing of the child thus Hannah's confidence in waiting until Samuel was weaned before taking him to Eli the priest.

REDEEM YOUR VOW

Hannah fulfilled her vow to the LORD, testified of God's blessing to Eli and gave her only child to God. Think about this, this was Hannah's long awaited first child whom she gave birth to after many years of grief and provocation. Even before she conceived she had promised to give the child to the Lord and she kept that promise. She was wise, she waited until the child was weaned [from breast milk so that her presence was not necessary for his upbringing], and not until he was much older by which time it would have been even harder for her to give him up. Verse 24 tells us Samuel was still very young when Hannah took him to Eli the priest, probably between three and five years of age depending on the tradition of those days. Even if you will not give your son to work in the ministry of the Lord, at least bring him up in the knowledge and fear of the Lord. You can't do better than that.

Redeeming one's pledge to God is essential.

My Personal Notes

Provocation, Prayer & Praise.

2

Rescued At 'Quarter To Shame'

In fulfilling her vow to God, Hannah came rejoicing and maybe dancing as she prayed what has become one of the most wonderful songs in the Bible:

> *"And Hannah prayed and said: "My heart rejoices in the Lord; my horn is exalted in the Lord. I smile at my enemies, because I rejoice in your salvation. There is none holy like the Lord, for there is none besides you, nor is there any rock like our God. Talk no more so very proudly; let no arrogance come from your mouth, for the Lord is the God of knowledge; and by Him actions are weighed.*
>
> *The bows of the mighty men are broken, and those who stumbled are girded with strength. Those who were full have hired themselves out for bread, and those who*

were hungry have ceased to hunger. Even the barren has borne seven, and she who has many children has become feeble. The Lord kills and makes alive; He brings down to the grave and brings up. The Lord makes poor and makes rich; He brings low and lifts up. He raises the poor from the dust and lifts the beggar from the ash heap, to set them among princes and make them inherit the throne of glory. For the pillars of the earth are the Lord's, and He has set the world upon them. He will guard the feet of His saints, but the wicked shall be silent in darkness. "For by strength no man shall prevail.

The adversaries of the Lord shall be broken in pieces; from heaven He will thunder against them. The Lord will judge the ends of the earth. "He will give strength to His king, and exalt the horn of His anointed." [1Samuel 2:1-10, NKJV]

Whatever is wrong, prayer can affect for change and whatever is good prayer is required to sustain. Hannah prayed before and after her desires were met.

Count Your Blessings Not Excuses

Now that Hannah had been blessed with Samuel, she still kept going to Shiloh. The blessing of God should not be an excuse for not worshipping or serving God or fellowshipping with other believers. Some say they are so busy taking care of the newborn child that they do not have time to read the Bible or even attend church services. They are either too tired or too busy. Let that not be your story. Hannah indeed went as far as making a robe for little Samuel every year, fulfilling her role as a responsible and thoughtful mother [v. 19].

This Too Will Pass

Eli specially blessed Elkanah and Hannah each time they came to the temple in Shiloh [v. 20]. Eli said because you have given Samuel to God, God will in turn grant you more children. In answer to these blessings uttered by Eli, God gave Hannah and Elkanah, three more sons and two daughters. What a mighty God we serve! Your present lack will turn into your future abundance when you pour your heart out to God. Giving usually precedes God's unlimited blessings. Give generously, for your gifts will return to you later [Ecclesiastes. 11:1, LB].

As you read further into chapter 25 of the book of 1 Samuel where we are told that Samuel died, you will find out that he became one of the highly esteemed prophets of God in the Bible and God was with him [1Samuel 3:19]. Many boys are still given the name Samuel. After all that taunting Hannah was subjected to in the hand of Peninnah, Peninnah and her children had to bring their requests and offerings through Samuel to God. When the Lord turns your shame and reproach around, your enemies and those who had despised you may be at your mercy needing your help.

Remember the well-known story of Joseph and his brothers [Genesis 50:15 -21]. Samuel here is an example of a child who got to know the Lord and began relating with Him at a very tender age until the time he died. Children can and are able to understand the Gospel message if we but teach them. Children don't lack intelligence; they simply lack teachers. Deuteronomy 6:7 (NLT) says "you must commit yourselves wholeheartedly to these commands that I am giving you today. Repeat them again and again to your children. Talk about them when you are at home and when you are on the road, when you are going to bed and when you are getting up". Some time ago a mother shared with me the fear of her 7-year-old daughter regarding a possible impending divorce between herself and the girl's father. Although this little girl was a Christian and prayed about her fear, she was very troubled by the state of affairs. I suggested to the mother that she take her daughter outside when it wasn't raining and ask her to choose any one of the clouds in the skies and keep her eyes on her chosen cloud and let her mother know when the cloud moves. I told the mother to use the moving cloud as an analogy for the young girl that problems will also move on and pass away just as the cloud does because God in His faithfulness would handle the situation in the best way possible.

She could also use the moon to remind her of God's faithfulness at all times because the moon does not fail to show up each evening. God provided the then 7-year girl another Godly father and she has since been happy.

God is timeless; He lives in eternity. Your miracle or blessing may not be made manifest just at the time you want it to but it will fulfil God's plan for your life and the world in His time. Delay is not necessarily denial. A woman of God once said 'God shows up, even at quarter to shame'

PARENTS ARE THEIR CHILDREN'S TEACHERS

Hannah gave God her son at a very early age. The greatest investment parents can give to their child is to teach and train them in the way of the LORD. Particularly before they start attending school where the world is waiting to bombard them with godless information. A parent can only give what he or she has. The problem is parents probably don't have much to give themselves. It is one thing to attend church regularly and participate actively and quite another to sincerely live for Christ. The teaching should not be left to the Sunday school teachers although they have a duty also but the main responsibility is that of the parents and it must not be shirked. It is a fallacy that young children cannot understand the message of the Gospel. Children do not lack capacity, I reiterate, they simply lack teachers. Don't get them to only draw and paint and sing and act, also teach them. When you use any of these activities, use them as teaching tools and not just to keep the children occupied until Sunday school is over or until you have 'time' for them. The aim is to ensure that your child knows God as Father, Jesus Christ as Saviour and more and the Holy Spirit as Helper. If this is achieved and the child desires to read the Bible and do what it says, you have succeeded in your bid to add another soul to the kingdom of heaven. Well done!

How do parents today prepare for the birth of a child? A lot of time is spent reading the available literature from medical books to children's magazines to attending parental classes in antenatal clinics. These are all very good but how many parents go further to prepare themselves spiritually? Some parents focus their prayers on the time of the pregnancy and labour but many may forget to ask God for divine wisdom in bringing up the child in the fear and nurture of the Lord. That is interesting because hardly will anyone send their child to a school where the teachers are untrained and with no teaching qualifications.

Parents really are the first teachers a child has. Yet many are unprepared for this life-long responsibility.

Organisations like Children's Evangelism Ministry [CEM], Focus on the Family and The Shepherd's Ministries [TSM] have affordable training programmes, which you can investigate and probably attend.

My Personal Notes

Provocation, Prayer & Praise.

3

THE POWER OF PRAYER

Your problem - its cause, duration and solution are absolutely in the hands of God. Dr Charles Stanley once said that God holds the thermostat to every believer's problems and trials. The temperature and duration are in God's full control.

Hannah was deeply distressed, and prayed to the LORD and wept bitterly. Infertility often brings deep distress, but it should lead us to seeking the LORD for help. Tears can be therapeutic whether you are a man or woman, young or old; pour out your heart to God, tell Him your feelings, hurts, fears, anxiety, etc.

Whatever brings you distress indeed is reason enough to pray.

ATTITUDE IS EVERYTHING

Hannah in humility referred to herself as a maidservant of God. With which attitude do you approach God? Jesus told this parable of two men who went to the temple to pray, the Pharisee prayed proudly, the other was sorry for his sins, but both prayed to God. Yet, only one went home forgiven and blessed [Luke 18: 9-14]. Attitude is almost everything, before God and before men. Human pride has no place with God; infact God loathes the proud person. See 1Peter 5:5.

Hannah sought God in the right place and with the right attitude not minding any one's interpretation of what she did. Eli got it really wrong; she was not drunk, quite a terrible accusation but Hannah answered the priest with the same humble attitude of spirit with which she prayed.

Hannah referred to her situation as an affliction. Whatever limitation you are facing or going through can be termed an affliction and requires help from God.

God is alive and well and sees you. HE knows and feels your affliction. See Exodus 3:7-8.

God's Covenant With Us

Hannah asked God to remember her. She wasn't asking God to remember her because He had forgotten her; she meant that God should put a mark on her as one desiring to have a child. We are the ones who need to remind ourselves of His covenant with us. The covenant of:

- His Word, which cannot fail [Numbers. 23:19, 2 Samuel. 22:31, Psalms. 119:49- 50, 89, 107, 140; 138:2, Proverbs. 30:15].
- The blood of Jesus, with which we were saved, made us His children [Hebrews. 10:22, 1 John 1:7].
- The name of Jesus at which every knee, every need, every issue including infertility must bow [Philippians. 2:90–11].
- The Holy Spirit our Helper and Guide [Jn. 14:26].
- Ministering angels who encamp around us [Matthew. 18:10, Psalms. 34:7].
- God has promised never to leave us or forsake us [Hebrews. 13:5b].

In verse 11 of 1 Samuel Chapter 1, Hannah's request was specific – she did not want just any child, she wanted God to give her 'a son'. How specific are you in your requests to God? God is more willing and eager to give than we know to receive. God will not withhold any good thing from us, as HE loves us so much HE gave us His only Son, Jesus Christ. As you ask for a child, a job or whatever the need, ask in faith [Hebrews 11:6].

Your problem may not be that of infertility like Hannah's, but whatever it is, trust in the Lord just as Hannah did, lean not on your own insight or understanding, in all your ways, acknowledge Him and HE will direct your paths [Proverbs 3:5-6].

WHY DO YOU WANT WHAT YOU WANT?

Why did Hannah want or need a child? Why do you want what you want? I don't think Hannah asked for a child so she could get even with Peninnah or just to show that she too could bear children and call herself a mother. Her vow to God silenced such speculations forever. Ask yourself, why do you want what you want? Is the reason to consume it on your own lusts as revealed in James 4:2-3? Consider this scripture and be honest in your answer.

Thank God for the Penninahs of this world whose provocations drive us closer to the LORD. Hannah prayed without reference to the provocateur. Neither did she wish evil on Peninnah. She had a need and focused on it in her prayer to God. She did not succumb to being vindictive and eventually, she was vindicated.

KEEP YOUR PLEDGE

Hannah made a vow to God – one that will take concerted consideration to keep. She was desperate and had counted the cost of making such a vow. What vow have you made to the LORD regarding that desire in your life? And if you made one, have you thought it out well enough; have you counted the cost of keeping it? Will you keep it?

It is far better not to say you'll do something than to say you will and then not do it. In that case, your mouth is making you sin. Don't try to defend yourself by telling the messenger from God that it was all a mistake [to make the vow]. That would make God very angry; and he might destroy your prosperity.

Dreaming instead of doing is foolishness, and there is ruin in a flood of empty words; fear God instead. [Ecclesiastes 5:5-6 LB]

Her vow was that her son would be consecrated and

given to the LORD, working in the temple all the days of his life. We were all created to worship God; we are saved to serve God, the body of CHRIST and the entire global community. This, therefore, was nothing new, nothing spectacular that Hannah would give her son to the service of the Lord except that it was her only and long awaited son and he was very young when she gave him to Eli. I have referred to this earlier on in the book. So would you put yourself in a position such as this considering the implications?

After Hannah had Samuel, she waited patiently until he was weaned before taking him to serve in the temple. In some instances, you might have to wait a little while after the need has been met before you are able to fulfill your vow. Once everything is in place for you to be able to fulfill your vow, would you still be willing to do so?

And when Hannah brought her son to the temple, she took with her offerings of a three-year old bull, an ephah (money) and a skin of wine to the house of the LORD at Shiloh. She testified to Eli the priest of what the Lord had done for her and left her son in his care.

Remember to bring an offering to the house of the LORD after testifying of what HE has done for you. There is power in sharing our testimony. Remember Revelation 12:11a.

Once again, Hannah prayed as in 1Samuel 2:1-10. Sing a new song unto the Lord for HE has done gloriously.

PS
In these days of modern technology and discoveries, there are many fertility treatments available to couples having difficulty conceiving naturally. Personally, I suggest that a couple having difficulty conceiving should first seek the face of God and once they are convinced that fertility treatment is the way forward for them and realising all that it entails, they should prayerfully embark on medical treatment knowing fully well that the experts can try but only God gives a child. It is not uncommon for a couple to naturally conceive just before embarking on fertility treatment or after failed attempts of fertility treatment. God will always remember His own in His own time.

My Personal Notes

Provocation, Prayer & Praise.

4

THE SOVEREIGNTY OF GOD

[This is a poem I wrote in February 1992 which I have included in the expectation that it will give you not just hope in a seemingly hopeless situation but it will also show you aspects of God's character as seen in His manifest abilities.]

MY UNLIMITED GOD

PART 1

MY GOD IS UNLIMITED in every way and at every time
How wonderful He is and marvellous in His dealings
with mankind
How faithful as He shows His love over and
over again to us
How timely are His interventions and accurate
are His judgements.

Imagine His unlimited wisdom in every known
creation of His
Imagine the vast knowledge awaiting human
discovery in every bit of life
Imagine the beauty, protection, and provision
for all living organisms
Imagine the complexity, uniqueness and
wonders in every life reproduced.

Think about His forgiveness to man with
wicked heart and intent
Think about His pardon of sin, no matter
how grievous at confession
Think about His restoration and love to all
– His prodigal children
Think about His cleansing that leaves
the sinner spotless and clean.

Remember His unlimited ways of speaking
to His own, His elect and anointed
Remember His revelations in dreams to
Jacob, Joseph, Pharaoh and Daniel
Remember His calling of Moses, Saul the King,
Saul of Tarsus and Simon Peter
Remember His visit to Abraham, Manoah's wife,
Gideon and Mary, Jesus' mother

Part 2

One can't forget His unique ways of healing
every form of disease encountered:
Healing of King Hezekiah by using a paste
made from dried figs
Healing of the paralytic man by the spoken
word of Christ the Messiah
Healing of Naaman the leper by seven
immersions in the River Jordan.

Healing of the man born blind by Jesus
applying mud to his eyes
Healing of the unrestrained man by casting
out the demons,
Healing of the centurion's servant by
word of command believed;
Healing of the woman with the issue of
blood by her touch of faith.

Healing of the Israelites of snake bites by
looking up at its replica;
Healing of Abimelech's household of infertility
by Abraham's prayer;

PROVOCATION, PRAYER & PRAISE.

Healing of the water causing miscarriages
by Elisha adding salt;
Healing from the poisoned meal by putting
some of it back into the pot.

Provision of forty years food for the
Israelites has never been equalled
Provision of food to starving Elijah by the
brook, through the ravens
Provision of food for the widow and her son,
through Elijah's words
Provision of better wine at the wedding
from water, very unique.

Leading of the Israelites to the Promised
Land, by His presence
Leading of the wise men to the promised
Child, by the lone bright star
Leading of the disciples to their assigned
duties, by the Holy Spirit
Leading of His children now, by the Scriptures
and the Holy Spirit.

The salvation of Zacchaeus' family, by Jesus'
invitation to Zacchaeus
The salvation of the jailer's family, by his
encounter with Paul and Silas

The salvation of Cornelius's family, by the
invitation of Simon Peter
Our salvation is by confession and
acceptance of His love by faith.

The final confirmation of a child to Abraham was
during the three men's visit
The deliverance of Lot and his family, by Lot's
kindness to the two strangers
The deliverance of the harlot and her family, by
her kindness to the two spies
The deliverance of mankind from Satan, sin and
death is by Christ's redemption.

The surgical provision of a wife to Adam, incredibly
remarkable
The faithful way He led Abraham's servant to
choose Rebecca, miraculous
The beginning of the marital relations between
Jacob and Rachel, unique
The leading of Moses to meet his future bride at a
well, amazing.

Part 3

Dear friend, is your god limited - in any place and at any time?
Is your god asleep, travelling, uncaring and unhelpful like Baal?
Is your god too weak and unable to defend himself like the smashed Baal?
Why not try my Unlimited God, the unique and everlasting Trinity?

PART 4

My Unlimited God is capable of handling
everysituation, however hard!
He is capable of fighting on your behalf,
without your fighting at all
He is capable of bounteous provision no
matter your need or want
He is capable of restoring all that
you have lost.

My Unlimited God is Father, Saviour,
Friend and Helper
He is undemanding, not like any of the gods you
have heard of anywhere and anytime
He is unselective in His love and mercies
toward mankind, no matter the colour
He is easily approachable - anytime, anywhere
and with any request.

My Unlimited God is caring- He knows each
of His own by name
He is concerned and so ordains every moment
and everyday of one's life

Provocation, Prayer & Praise.

He is conscious of every sparrows fall and
all mankind's needs.

He is accurate as HE never sleeps nor
slumbers or forgets His promises.
My unlimited God is everlasting, ever-present
and always ready
He is known in every part of the world and
through history
He is unlimited in His presence and power
He is constant in this changing, unstable,
unpredictable world of ours.

My unlimited God cannot be restricted
by unbelief, doubt or fear
He is unlimited in any situation in which
man mayfind himself
He is unlimited in the love bestowed on
each lost one
He is unlimited in His ability to bring the
best out of the worst and weak.

My unlimited God can never be faulted
by any known science or technology
He cannot be accused of injustice, corruption,
deceit, or unfaithfulness
He cannot be overruled by any judge,
king, force, power, or atomic bomb

The Sovereignty Of God

He cannot be questioned or asked to render
an account or explanation.

My unlimited God can never be deceived
by anyone at anytime
For He sees right through into every human
heart, thought and intent
He knows the end of all before the beginning,
how great He is!
He hears every unsaid, whispered or shouted
discussion and prayer.

Part 5

He answers prayers properly directed
to Him in faith
He answers some while we are still thinking
about phrasing them
He answers others long after we have prayed
and sometimes forgotten
My unlimited God is a faithful, unfailing, caring
and prayer-answering God!

GOD'S GIFT YOU CAN NEVER BUY

Beloved have you ever thought about something?
I mean about God's numerous gifts to mankind?
Isn't God wonderful and generous to you and me?
All His gifts to mankind, He gave free of charge.

Beginning with life itself, is free to mankind
Money can buy good medicine and care but not life or health
The air we breathe in is abundant and free
Can you imagine if we have to pay for that in a day?

Nothing quenches thirst as much as ordinary water
Yet in abundance, God has made it available to man
The radiant sun breaks the dawn and shines bright
All living things depend on it for their growth and vitality.

That pretty baby is a wonderful gift from God
Medicine can help produce test tube babies
Yet the sperm and egg are really God's
Indeed God's gift you and I can never buy.

Provocation, Prayer & Praise.

Imagine Jesus having to pay the heavy price for our sins
On the cross, He was hanged for you and me
Shedding His innocent and sinless blood
For there is none else qualified for the atonement required.

What on earth is equivalent to the shed blood?
What can we pay for such an eternal sacrifice?
Who among the prophets could stand in the gap?
To appease God's wrath and justice against man.

Tell me which power is equal to that of the Holy Spirit
Who is as humble and powerful as Him?
Yet at Pentecost, He was poured on the disciples
And today, He is still empowering Christians.

Simon the sorcerer thought he could buy salvation
And possibly a bit of the Holy Ghost manifestations
He asked the apostles for it, offering some money
How he could have thought such gift can be bought.

Haven't we in previous times tried to buy some of God's gifts?
By the very way we think and live our lives
Why not pause and think when next you are tempted
There is no controversy, God's gift you can never buy.

There are not enough riches in the world, the Bible says
To redeem just a single soul from hell fire
There are not enough blankets or scientific discoveries
To cover the glory of the most tiny star in the sky
There is no controversy, God's gift you can never buy
Indeed God's gift you can never buy.
© *Ola- Ojo 1991/92*

THE LORD IS WORKING

The Lord is working but we may not know it
He works in all places at all times for all people
He quietly works His way and plan many times unnoticed
However slow it seems to be, God is continuously working.

As much as He works day and night,
He is never tired
For He never sleeps nor slumbers, never weary nor weak
He never gets mixed up with people, problems or situations
Neither is He disturbed, worried, fretful or forgetful.

The Lord is working even though we may not physically see Him
He is continuously working in us, for us, with us and everywhere

His work does not have to do with whether we love Him or not
It has nothing to do either with our loyalty or disloyalty to Him.

He created all things and has sustained them all over the ages
He has organised His creatures to do certain things at specific times
Human beings He gave the free will to do as each of us like
He has made mankind in His image and likeness.

The sun rises and sets at the right times year in year out
The moon and the stars give their lights in the night unfailingly
The winds blow to and fro and the clouds are always there
The rain and snow come at their specified seasons.

The trees grow and produce fruits according
to their season
The birds sing sweet early morning songs
without fail
The flowers blossom in their own season
beautifully
While the animals keep to their different
territories.

The baby in the mother is formed under God's
supervision
He knows *him from the womb and has
ordained him from birth
Everyday of each person's life He has pre
recorded in His book
How busy the Lord must be to keep trail of all
that happens.

His eyes run throughout the whole world every
time of each day.
Watching particularly His own, those whose
hearts are stayed on Him
His ears are never weary to listen to
everybody everywhere and every time
How great He must be to understand all
creatures' languages.

My brother, my sister the Lord is still working
for you
He will certainly make all things work together
for your good
No matter how terrible, confusing or
frightening the situation is
Be assured the Lord is concerned and working
right now on it.

© Ola- Ojo 8/8/89 based on Psalms 9:13, 139: 13-16 and Romans 8:28.

*him – used for both gender.

Whom Are You Listening To In That Situation?

Brother in that difficult situation you are in
In that challenging phase you are going through
In that nerve wrecking vocation you are in
In that turbulent marriage you have found yourself
Whom are you listening to I dare to ask you?

Perhaps you have consulted the experts to your problem
Perhaps you have been to see the best doctors or surgeons
Perhaps you have visited herbalists or mediums
Perhaps you have made appointments to speak to counsellors
What have they told you and whom are you listening to?

What you hear can positively or negatively influence you
Whom you continue to listen to will definitely affect you

What and whom you have contacted will leave deposits in you
What and whom you choose to believe will affect you
What have you been told and whom are you listening to?

The best of the experts findings are just facts
The best of the counsellor's wisdom is very limited
The best of foreseeing by the mediums and herbalists are lies
The best of medical findings are facts subject to a change from God
What facts have you now and whom are you listening to?

Some people will come to tell lies and halftruths for their own profit
Some people will come and tell you stories that make you sadder
Some people will fabricate stories so as to take advantage of your situation
Some people will do anything to make your relationship not to work
What have people been telling you and whom are you listening to?

To live in peace and flourish in the same
situation you are in now
Calls for you to choose very prayerfully who
you listen to
Calls for you to take all information back to
God in prayers
Calls for you to remain focused on God even in
that situation
For whom and what you listen to are very important.

Facts, lies, half-truths from even the best
quarters are dangerous
Listening to tale bearers whoever they are, is
a subtle way of self destruction
Visiting herbalists and mediums is unjustifiable
and against God
Seek the LORD with all your heart and let God
speak to.

Whom are you listening to; I dare to ask you
in the name of the LORD?

©O.Ola-Ojo 16.08.04

MY FAITH IS BEING PUT TO TEST.

Many times in life I do not understand
Why I have to pass through difficult times
Sometimes having to work with difficult people
Sometimes having to live with difficult people
Sometimes having to have difficult experiences
But like the man of God rightly mentioned
My faith is being put to test through them all.

I may not be able to explain to anyone
What pains I have suffered in this life
What trials and difficulties I have gone through
What hardships I have faced as a person
What burdens have remained unburdened?
What temptations I have been subjected to
As my faith is being put to test in all.

I perfectly admit how I feel all these while I
personally confess how I feel like at such times
I happily admit God's goodness even in them
I totally refuse to condemn You Lord or myself
I knowingly believe in Your love and faithfulness
I absolutely put my total confidence in You alone
As my faith is constantly being put to test.

I am going to allow God alone to have His way
To make the best of all these situations
To grant me enough grace to sail through
Or to transform the situations to His Glory
No matter how soon or how late God may be
To come to my aid in all these respects I believe
My own situation is never helpless or hopeless.

© Ola - Ojo '89. Psalms 56: 2-4, 9b - 11.

My Personal Notes

Provocation, Prayer & Praise.

Song

WHAT A FRIEND WE HAVE IN JESUS

What a friend we have in Jesus
All our sins and griefs to bear?
What a privilege to carry
Everything to God in prayer!
Oh what peace we often forfeit
Oh what needless pain we bear
All because we do not carry
Everything to God in prayer.

Have we trials and temptations
Is there trouble anywhere?
We should never be discouraged
Take it to the LORD in prayer
Can we find a friend so faithful?
Who will all our sorrows share?
Jesus knows our every weakness
Take it to the LORD in prayer.

Are we weak and heavy laden?
Cumbered with a load of care?
Precious Saviour still our refuge
Take it to the Lord in prayer

Do thy friends despise, forsake thee?
Take it to the Lord in prayer
In His arms He'll take and shield thee
Thou wilt find a solace there.

Joseph Scriven 1820 – 1886.
Hymn of Glorious Praise 1969 Copyright by Gospel Publishing House USA

OPPORTUNITY TO BECOME A CHRISTIAN

Dear Father in heaven,
Thank you for the privilege of reading this book. 'Indeed I have sinned and come short of Your glory.' I am grateful to You for sending Jesus Christ into this world to come to die on the cross of Calvary for me. I believe in my heart that Jesus Christ paid for my sins, past, present and future. I believe Jesus Christ was buried and on the third day He rose from the dead. I believe that Jesus Christ will come back again. I confess with my mouth and I accept Him now to be my Lord.

Master, Saviour, Brother, and Friend. I ask in Your mercy for the infilling of the Holy Spirit so that with His help, I can live a victorious life becoming all that You have ordained me to be in Jesus' name I pray with thanksgiving.
Amen.

*If after reading this book you said the above prayer and became born-again, 'Congratulations! You are Born Again' is a booklet for those who have done so through reading this book. It is a free booklet that we would like you to have. In it, the frequently asked questions are answered and this will get you on the way to growing in your newfound faith in God. You can download this free booklet from our website:
www.protokospublishers.com
You may also contact any of the organisations
listed at the end of the book.
I look forward to hearing from you soon.
O. Ola –Ojo (2009)*

Dads, Mums And Miracle Tots Support Group

It dawned on me as I wrote that there might be a lot more than I can imagine of women and men around the world who have similar problems to that of Hannah's that I have also written extensively about in one of my other books, Provocation, Prayer and Praise – (see preview at the back of book).

This thought grew until I came to crossroads as to whether it was a good idea to form a Support Group for such persons. I took a right turn and decided that it would be a wonderful initiative.

The idea is this: it is an avenue for would-be Dads and Mums to be comforted and supported. This can be done through many means possible. A thought is to share your experiences with one another and hopefully glean some wisdom too.

The group is open to couples who have had fertility treatment in the past or are currently going through fertility treatment or considering fertility treatment for whatever reason, professionals in the fertility field, (although no professional consultation will be offered), those who believe in prayers and in praying and are willing and able to support these potentially fruitful couples.

The aim is not necessarily to 'meet' physically every week or even every month. You will have to be registered on our website *www.protokospublishers.com* to share your experiences, receive encouraging poems, prayer requests and praise items.

I hope this will prove to be a huge success for everyone involved. Please write me and let me know what you think.

May the blessing of being fruitful and multiplying be yours in Jesus' name.

Your sister,

O. OLA-OJO

OTHER BOOKS BY THE AUTHOR:

Provocation, Prayer and Praise
(December 2004 & 2009)

Complimentary to The Christian and Infertility this book focuses on the story of an infertile woman in the Bible, her provocations, prayer and praise. Whatever makes you incomplete, unfulfilled, less than whom God made you to be, whatever issue of life that the enemy uses to provoke you calls for prayer.

Key features include:
- Some known medical reasons for infertility in the women.
- Why Hannah went to the house of God in spite of her barrenness.
- Is it true that the husband is much more than 10 sons to the infertile woman?
- When, where and how to address the source/cause of your provocation.
- God's part and your part in that promise.
- God is able to met that humanly impossible need of yours.
- A time to celebrate and praise God.

Book Details:
Paperback: 128 pages
Language English
ISBN-13: 978-0-9557898-3-0

A Reader from London, 7 Jan 2006 on Amazon.co.uk
An excellent easy to read and understand book. The principles shared in this book though primarily are for those trying for a baby could as well be applied to any area of hurt and un-fulfilment.

 :www.protokospublishers.com

The Christian and Infertility
(December 2004 & 2009)

The Christian and Infertility addresses one of the often neglected needs of Christian couples. It gives an insight into infertility from the biblical and medical perspectives. It is written not only for potential fruitful couples but for pastors, family and friends of these couples. It is written that the Body of Christ might be fully equipped to know and support couples who are facing the challenge of infertility at present.

Key features include:
- Childleness in the Bible and lessons to learn;
- Some possible physical, medical and environmental causes of infertility;
- Some known spiritual causes of infertility;
- The man and low sperm count;
- Some of the available treatment optons in the UK;
- Choice of fertility treatment;
- Should a christian professional be involved in fertility treatment?

Book Details:
Paperback: 146 pages
Language English
ISBN-13: 978-0-9557898-2-3

*A reviewer from Glen Burnie, USA, 29 Oct 2007 on Amazon.co.uk'
The book is a great eye-opener for all. It sheds light on infertility from the medical and spiritual angle. This gives the reader a balance because i believe every human being is made up of both physical and spiritual part. To get a balance in life, the two parts must be well fed. One must not concentrate on the spiritual and neglect the physical part. The book also reminds us that God has a way of sorting us out.... The book is quite inspiring. I will recommend this book to everybody trusting God for any form of blessing from God to go get one and apply it to his or her situation. It will definitely bless you and yours'.*

 :www.protokospublishers.com

Obstetrics and Gynaecology Ultrasound - A Self-Assessment Guide

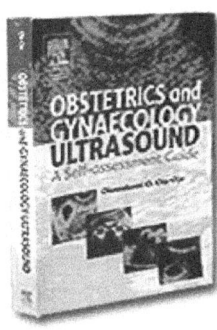

June 2005 Churchill Elsevier Publishers, UK.

This self-assessment guide is a structured questions and answer book that develops the reader's understanding capability using a simple method in treating related topics. Clinical indications are presented with their corresponding ultrasound findings using appropriate illustrations. A case study approach is followed; presenting the clinical and ethical dilemmas that might arise whilst encouraging students to think. The aim is to reinforce theoretical knowledge within a clinical environment.

Key features:
- Over 600 high-resolution ultrasound images
- Cover a wide spectrum of ultrasound curriculum.
- Includes a detailed study of fertility.
- Aids quick understanding of subject matter.
- 468 pages.

ISBN-10: 0443064628
ISBN-13: 978-0443064623
Book Dimensions: 24 x 16.8 x 2.6 cm

"...This excellent new book is a study guide... This is an attractive paperback that should be essential reading for trainee obstetric and gynaecological sonographers, whether they are radiographers or radiology or obstetric trainees. It will be of particular value to those preparing for the RCOG/RCR Diploma in Advanced Obstetric Ultrasound and to specialist registrars in obstetrics and gynaecology undertaking special skills modules in fetal medicine, gynaecological ultrasound and infertility..."

The Obstetrician & Gynaecologist, www.rcog.org.uk/togonline
Book reviews 2006

Reviewer **Ann Harper MD FRCPI FRCOG.**
Consultant Obstetrician and Gynaecologist
Royal Jubilee Maternity Service, Belfast., UK

 :www.protokospublishers.com

GOOD MUMS, BAD MUMS
(June 2005 & 2009)

This is in two parts, the main chapter that can be used for personal or group study, and an accompanying exercise section. The privileged position of a mother is in her being a co-creator with God and bringing forth life (lives). This book compliments one of God's previous revelations to me as contained in the book titled Good Dads, Bad Dads'. Whilst the father could be likened to the pilot of the family plane, the mother can be likened to the force behind the plane – positive or negative. Good mothers are not only co-creators with God, they also do nurture as well as nourish their children physically, emotionally and spiritually.

Keys Features:
- Were all the mothers in the Bible god mothers?
- Lessons from the strengths and weakness of seven mothers.
- Be encouraged - you are not alone in the assignment of motherhood.
- Be motivated in the areas of your strengths.
- Learn ways of supporting your husband and children.

Book Details:
Paperback: 162 pages
Language English
ISBN-13: 978-0-9557898-1-6
Book Dimensions: 21.4 x 14 x 1.4 cm

 :www.protokospublishers.com

To the Bride with Love
(2007 & 2009)

Every wise woman preparing to get married knows she will need sound advice, practical tips and solid, heartfelt prayers, of those who have travelled on the road she is about to journey on. In this book, 10 women of different age groups, from different backgrounds and cultures who wedded under various circumstances, individually share their experience with the bride in an intimate, very candid and unforgettable way.

Book details:
Paperback: 108 pages
Language English
ISBN-13: 978-0-9557898-4-7
Book Dimensions: 22.4 x 15 x 1 cm

To the Bride with Love is the perfect bride's evergreen companion. The content is suitable, relevant and applicable even decades after the wedding day.
To the Bride with Love is an ideal wedding gift on its own. It can also accompany any other gift (big or small) that you have for the bride but take this hint... the bride will keep thanking you for the book years and years after.

'One of the best', 19 Jul 2008 on Amazon.com
Sade Olaoye "clare4good" (United Kingdom)
This book has really helped my marriage from the onset as I got it as a wedding gift, God bless the giver. It's a must read fro relationship improvement and God's guidance. I recommend people to get for oneself and also as a great blessing for someone else in love. "To the Bride with Love"

Provocation, Prayer & Praise.

Review by Oyinlola Odunlami CEO.
Shallom Bookshop, London UK

The writing style of Oluwakemi is unique, peculiar and distinct to herself. I recommend To the Bride with Love to wives, wives to be, mothers, mentors, youth leaders and workers. Why? The clarity, the focus and the intent of this book is so empowering, encouraging and enlightening that it will definitely mould or re mould a life to achieve its purpose. The truth is, there are very few books that have depth as well as help you to achieve your goals and arrive at your destination. Many books tend to excite you but have no depth; you read and you forget; they do not really change you but this book, To the Bride with Love will definitely leave a word in your spirit and move you to your next level!

I believe that this is also a book that pastors will find useful as a manual for marriage counselling, because many books on marriage focus mostly on what you as an individual can gain, your own personal satisfaction while little is said about the sacrifices involved and their importance. As my pastor usually says, it is important to learn from those who have gone ahead, understand why some were successful and others weren't, so that we won't fall where they fell, rather, we would gain more speed, achieve our goals and thereby glorify Christ.

So, I invite you not only to get a copy of this life-changing manual for yourself, but also to put it into as many hands as you can afford to, for then the world will definitely benefit and your life will be a blessing to many.

 :www.protokospublishers.com

PROVOCATION, PRAYER & PRAISE.

Refuge Under His Wings

"an exhaustive analysis of the Book of Ruth in the Bible. The author combines her deep Christian conviction and excellent knowledge of the Holy Scriptures to produce a must read for every Christian, married or single. The book is interspaced with beautifully written prayers, which enables the reader to pause, pray and meditate on the revelations received... The book is also loaded with poetry like 'Thy will be done oh Lord' for those who may be facing an uncertain future or on a cross road of decisions."

Dr E B Ekpo MD, FRCP
Queen Elizabeth Hospital, Christian Fellowship,
Woolwich, London. UK

"...[a] ...spiritually sound book... a fine work of thoughtful reading and study...
I therefore recommend it to every Christian, married or single....
Pat Roach Senior Pastor
New Covenant Church.
Wandsworth Branch, London. UK.

Book details:
Paperback: 100 pages
Language English
ISBN-10: 095578980X
ISBN-13: 978-0955789809

This book feeds the soul. Most of all I loved the poetry. It gives you time to savour the thoughts as reader. There is a good mix of poetry and prose.To look at the story of Ruth in depth gave good spiritual food. You can pause and take it in at your own pace.The meditation on Psalm 121 was good also. There's nothing like reading a Psalm slowly and meditating on its contents. The author's own reflections allow you to see the book through someone else's eyes. A good read.

Book Review: by **Gaby Richards**, London, UK.

 :www.protokospublishers.com

USEFUL ADDRESSES:

Aglow International
Website: www.aglow.org
Aglow International is a network of caring women, a faith-building organisation rooted in local groups and international in scope, yet one-on-one in ministry. Their mission is to lead women to Jesus Christ and provide opportunity for Christian women to grow in their faith and minister to others.

Care for the Family
PO Box 488
Cardiff
CF15 7YY
Tel: (029) 2081 0800
Fax: (029) 2081 4089
Email: mail@cff.org.uk
Website: www.care-for-the-family.org.uk OR www.cff.org.uk
Care for the Family aims to promote strong family life and to help those hurting because of family breakdown. Their heart is to come alongside people in the good times and in the tough times - bringing
hope, compassion and some practical, down-to-earth help and encouragement.

Children Evangelism Ministry Inc
P.O. Box 4480
Ilorin, Kwara State,
Nigeria.
Tel: +234 31 222199
E-mail: cem@ilorin.skannet.com OR cem562000@yahoo.com
Children Evangelism Ministry Inc is a ministry that reaches out with the Gospel to children before and after birth. The ministry teaches and equips parents, teachers and coordinators of Sunday Schools and Children's Clubs. They also have and hold Children's Clubs,
conferences and training seminars.

Focus on the Family
Tel: 1-800 - 232 6459
Website: www.family.org
Focus on the Family cooperates with the Holy Spirit in disseminating the Gospel of Jesus Christ to as many people as possible, and specifically, to accomplish that objective by helping to preserve traditional values and the institution of the family.

HFEA
Website: www.hfea.org or www.hfea.gov.uk
Human Fertilisation & Embryology Authority. *An organisation in the United Kingdom that regulates and monitors all aspects of Fertility treatments, egg, sperm and embryo storage. They also have 'The HFEA guide to Infertility 2007/08' – in this free magazine are many relevant articles that you might find helpful.*

The Shepherd's Ministries
5 Brookehowse Road
Bellingham
London SE6 3TJ, UK
Tel/Fax: +44 208 698 7222
Email: info@theshepherdsministries.org
Website: www.theshepherdsministries.org
The Shepherd's Ministries helps to bring children into an experience of worshipping God in truth and in spirit; give children a world-view based on God's word and mission and helps children to exercise their gifts in local and global missions.

Total Woman Ministries
The Total Woman Ministries,
3 Herringham Road
Thames Wharf Barrier,
Charlton,
London
SE7 8NJ.

Tel: 020 8293 3730
Fax: 020 8293 3731
Email: admin@totalwomanministries.org
Website: www.totalwomanministries.org

Total Woman Ministries by God's grace has the sole vision of reaching out to women of all categories (married, single, separated / divorced, young, middle-aged or elderly).

USEFUL WEB-SITES:

Embryo adoption:
www.womens-health.co.uk/embryo_donation.html
http://www.babycentre.co.uk
www.EmbryoAdoption.org
www.nightlight.org/snowflakeadoption.html
www.lifefocus.tv
www.embryosalive.com

HFEA:
www.hfea.org
www.hfea.gov.uk – Donor Anonymity

Infertility Network:
http://www.infertilitynetworkuk.com

Protokos Publishers:
www.protokospublishers.com

Dear Reader,

Thank you for your time and resources committed to supporting this writing ministry. Please help to tell others about how much the Lord has blessed you reading this book.

You will certainly be blessed by the other books written by Oluwakemi, so why not visit www.protokospublishers.com and place an order today.

It will equally be appreciated if you can help to write a few sentences review of the book on www.amazon.com and / or on www.protokospublishers.com.

Please note that all our books are easily available from our website.

God bless you as you do.
Management
Protokos Publishers.

www.ingramcontent.com/pod-product-compliance
Lightning Source LLC
Chambersburg PA
CBHW051456290426
44109CB00016B/1774